my Texas garden

a gardener's journal

To: Lea,
May all your
gardening notes
be great!
Dale Groom
9-9-00

Dale Groom

Copyright © 2000 Dale Groom

All rights reserved. No part of this book may be reproduced or transmitted in any form or by any means, electronic or mechanical, including photocopying, recording, or by any information storage or retrieval system, without permission from the publisher.

ISBN 1-930604-02-5

NOTE: The ideas expressed in this book are not, in all cases, exact quotations, as some have been edited to fit the format. In all cases, the publisher has attempted to maintain the speaker's original intent. Further, in some cases, source materials for this book were obtained from secondary sources, primarily print media and the Internet. While every effort has been made to ensure the accuracy of these sources, accuracy cannot be guaranteed. To notify us of any corrections or clarifications, please contact Cool Springs Press.

Cool Springs Press, Inc.
112 Second Avenue North
Franklin, TN 37064

First Printing 2000
Printed in the United States of America
10 9 8 7 6 5 4 3 2 1

Design by: Sheri Ferguson
Illustrations by: Allison Starcher
Editorial Consultant: Erica Glasener

Visit the Cool Springs Press website at www.coolspringspress.com

a gardener's journal

this is my

Texas

garden

_____
name

_____
year

why keep a garden journal ?

Welcome! We Texas gardeners have wonderful opportunities for creating a variety of gardens. The state is quite diverse as far as soils and climate zones are concerned. Needless to say, there is a large collection of plants available to us as we begin to create beautiful gardens. We also know there are many elements to balance in order to garden successfully. That is why you will enjoy *My Texas Garden: A Gardener's Journal*.

Keeping a garden journal will help you keep track of how your garden grows. You will discover which plants thrive, which ones struggle, and best of all, you will discover many surprises. More than just record keeping, journaling is a way to trace your growth as a gardener. Writing down your favorite moments in the garden may help you decide which plants to add or which to replace. How does your garden make you feel? You may discover you prefer one season to another. Maybe your style of gardening has changed. A journal will help you track the evolution of your garden.

As gardeners know, weather is a huge factor in plant performance. By keeping track of air temperature, the amount of rainfall, and drastic changes (storms or droughts), we can see which plants survived and plan better for next year.

Has the environment in your garden changed? Trees and shrubs that were once small may have matured and created a shadier garden. Keeping a list of what you plant, where and when you plant it, and the source of the plant will provide useful information for the future.

Further, keeping up with what's blooming when, and how long is another reason to take time to write daily or weekly in this garden journal. You might be surprised at how many seasons your garden features beautiful blooms, colorful foliage, or fantastic fruits. Some of the best color combinations happen by accident and remembering which plant blooms and when it blooms from year to year is not easy. But with good journal records, you may recreate pleasing plant combinations and avoid repeating mistakes.

How often you fertilize, prune, and water are other things to keep track of in your garden journal. Which techniques have been most successful? If you have a particular pest or disease problem with one plant, what methods were effective in eradicating or controlling the problem? If your roses were beautiful last year, when did you prune them and how much did you prune? When did you divide your phlox and where did you plant the different varieties of spring bulbs? All of these questions can be answered in the pages of *My Texas Garden*.

getting started with your garden journal

By keeping daily records, you can check your journal and chart your most successful garden practices. Whether it's how and when you propagated a favorite hydrangea or rose, when the first bluebonnets came into bloom, or the scent of a particular native vine, your Texas garden journal will provide the ideal format for keeping in touch with your garden and what it can teach you. Here's how to begin.

- Designate a day and a time to write in your journal. You might discover that early morning coffee time or the end of the day works best.
- Use a favorite pen and keep it with your journal. Write brief, clear notes (*rainy and cool with temp around 60° F, daffodils and jonquils are in bloom. Redbud and dogwood trees are starting to open. Planted a 10-gallon 'Oklahoma' redbud on the east side of the house*).
- Keep a 5"x 7" envelope tucked in the back of your journal to hold photographs and pictures from catalogues or magazines that inspire you. Be sure to identify and label pictures.
- List existing trees, shrubs, perennials, and bulbs, including a sketch of where they are located. This will be especially helpful over the years when you make changes in your garden.

Once you get used to journaling, you may find that you look forward to writing about your garden as much as you enjoy adding new plants.

{ introduction }

Texas has five different climactic zones. The state reaches from zone 6 in the Panhandle where minus 10°F is common, all the way down to zone 9 in the valley where freezes are uncommon. There is no other state in the country that has this diversity. Temperatures in urban areas can be 10 degrees warmer than those in rural areas due to asphalt, concrete, masonry, and a denser population—all of which create microclimates.

Microclimates can also be created in our home landscapes by fencing, shrubbery, and by our homes and structures. You may discover that your yard has a location where particular plants will survive due to a microclimate that you have created while your neighbor may not be able to grow the same plants.

Study the environmental conditions in your garden and let the garden tell you what to do. Familiarize yourself with the native or indigenous plants of your region. If you like their looks and growth habits, use some of them as a guide to selections for your garden—both native and non-native. Knowing the type of soil, light, and exposure your plants require will help you select the right plant for the right place. With the exception of large trees and shrubs, don't be afraid to move your plants. Often conditions change, and what was once a favorable environment may no longer be. Proper watering, mulching, and fertilizing further help to ensure the success of your garden.

A problem that we often encounter when plants are brought in from parts of the country where summers are mild is damage by our prolonged high summer temperatures.

When you read that particular plants can grow in full sun, make sure the writer is referring to full sun in Texas.

the plan

It usually is useful to consult a professional garden designer or landscape architect to help you plan your garden. Their work can be as detailed as a drawing with every plant sited or as simple as a list of recommended plants for particular areas. After moving into a new home, begin visiting local nurseries, parks, arboreta, botanic gardens, etc., to help familiarize yourself with plants that perform well locally. These visits will help you determine which areas in your property to plant with specific plants to maximize your efforts. I also recommend that you acquire a copy of my book, *Dale Groom's Texas Gardening Guide* (Cool Springs Press, 1997). Its pages are filled with information for Texans and list specific plants that grow well here. Once you have a plan, you can implement it in stages over time. And, making adjustments as conditions or your tastes change is easy. For answers to specific questions, you may e-mail me at: plantgrm@cleaf.com.

soil

I've often said, "Soil is the foundation for successful gardening experiences. Take care of it so it can help you achieve your own personal gardening goals." Before planting anything in your home landscape, be sure you understand the soil that you have, and prepare that soil. It is important that you know whether you have well-drained soil, sandy soil, clay soil, etc. Before planting, prepare the soil by breaking it up in some way. The incorporation of organic matter will greatly improve the soil's drainage and moisture-and nutrient-holding capacity.

amending your soil

Compost is one of the best soil amendments because it is alive with billions of creatures to help roots absorb water and nutrients. Decomposed leaves, lawn clippings, pruned branches, and discarded plant parts harbor the beneficial fungi, bacteria, and other living creatures that are important parts of healthy soil. Making compost can be as simple as piling leaves and clippings in a heap and letting them break down. You can use 3 inches or more of quality organic matter blended with native Texas soils when preparing for bedding plants.

Our trees require a simple loosening of the soil. In most cases, it is impossible to amend the soil in an area wide enough or deep enough for a tree's root system. Simply loosen the soil thoroughly before planting your trees, and be sure you have selected the right trees for your soil type.

watering

Watering seems like a simple thing, but gardeners have a tendency to overwater or underwater. There are some plants that require very little water but others must be moist at all times. Water your plants deeply and thoroughly when they need it. Lawns need to be watered a minimum of 6 inches deep, and they prefer to be watered as far as 8 inches. After watering, don't water again until your plants tell you they need it. You can tell when your shrubs need to be watered by simply sticking your finger in the soil. If the soil is dry, apply water thoroughly. Lawns change from normal green to a blue-gray color, grass blades will roll or curl on their edges or the grass will not spring back after foot traffic if suffering from moisture stress. If any of these signs occur, soak the lawn thoroughly. Early morning is the best time to apply water in Texas.

guidelines for watering:
- Water your container plants until the water runs out the bottom. During hot summer months some containers may need water twice a day. Do not water until the top inch of the soil is dry to the touch.
- Put a hose at the base of a newly installed tree or shrub and thoroughly soak the rootball as needed. As the plant grows, the area that needs to be soaked will increase as the root zone increases.

- Drip irrigation is the most efficient method of delivering water to landscape plants including trees, shrubs, vines, groundcovers, annuals, and perennials.
- Buy an inexpensive water timer and a few soaker hoses. They are a worthwhile investment. During periods of drought mature trees will benefit from long, slow watering, especially during July, August, and maybe September.

mulch

Mulch acts like a blanket, holding moisture in the soil and keeping the soil temperatures from getting too hot or too cold. Mulch is most important for conserving water and can also help reduce weed infestations.

tips when mulching:

- Apply a 3-4 inch layer of mulch on top of the soil around all plants.
- Pine bark mulch, shredded leaves, pine bark nuggets, hardwood bark, pine straw, and clean hay are good choices.

nutrients

The main nutrients plants need are nitrogen, phosphorous, and potassium. When you buy fertilizer you will see three numbers on the bag representing the percentage of each nutrient in the mixture. For example, a bag of 15-5-10 fertilizer contains 15% nitrogen (N), 5% phosphorus (P), and 10% potassium (K). The other 70% is a carrier to distribute the fertilizer.

Each nutrient serves a function in the overall good health of a plant. Nitrogen promotes leaf growth, and the green color so often desired.

That is why lawn fertilizer has a high nitrogen percentage. Phosphorous is important in the formation of roots as well as flower, seed, and fruit growth. That is why starter fertilizers and bloom fertilizers have high percentages of phosphorous. Potassium increases overall cell health. When plants are under stress from drought or cold, adequate potassium helps the plant withstand the crisis.

soil test

A soil test helps determine how much fertilizer to apply and whether additives (such as lime, sulphur, or iron) are needed. It is worth performing the soil test every two years. You may have it tested through the Texas Agricultural Extension Service. This office is usually located in the county courthouse, county annex, or another county office location.

Lime and other pH-adjusting additives help plants absorb nutrients. Adding lime helps make soils less acidic and more alkaline. Adding sulphur and iron reduces the alkalinity, thus making soils more acid. Soil acidity and alkalinity is measured in numbers from 1 to 14 on the pH scale. Most plants prefer a soil that has a pH of 6.0 to 6.5. Below 7 is an acidic soil, and above 7 is an alkaline soil. Your soil test will determine the pH of your soil and the amount of any additives needed.

get started journaling and have fun

Your garden is what you make it. If you keep your heart and mind open to the nuances of nature, you will cultivate more than just pretty flowers and strong trees. You, your family, and your plants will grow in your beautiful garden. Remember, gardens are wonderful places to spend quality time, and to share productive and enjoyable times with those we love the most…our families. And there's nothing better in the world than growing a family together. So, to you and yours, "Have fun and GREAT GARDENING!"

Texas Garden Favorites

I selected a list of plants that are normally easy to grow, readily available, adaptable to various growing conditions, and help provide year-round interest in Texas landscapes and gardens. These plants can be very beneficial to your Texas garden because they provide brilliant color, some attract birds and wildlife, and most require minimal maintenance. You will find all of these recommendations in my book *Dale Groom's Texas Gardening Guide* (Cool Springs Press, 1997). Give these a try!

Annuals

- Bachelor Buttons — *Gomphrena globosa*
- Salvia — *Salvia coccinea*
- Copper Plant — *Acalypha wilkesiana*
- Periwinkle — *Catharanthus roseus*
- Pansy — *Viola* x *wittrockiana*
- Zinnia — *Zinnia elegans*
- Sunflower — *Helianthus annuus*
- Petunia — *Petunia* x *hybrida*

Perennials

- Lantana — *Lantana montevidensis*
- Mexican Petunia — *Ruellia brittoniana*
- Four-o-Clocks — *Mirabilis jalapa*
- Garden Mum — *Dendranthema* cultivars
- Dusty Miller — *Centaurea ceneraria*
- Southernwood — *Artemisia abrotanum*
- Yarrow — *Achillea* cultivars
- Pinks — *Dianthus* spp.

Bulbs, corms, tubers and rhizomes

- Iris — *Iris* spp.
- Canna — *Canna* x *generalis*
- Crinum — *Crinum* spp.
- Daylily — *Hemerocallis* spp.
- Caladium — *Caladium* x *hortulanum*
- Narcissus — *Narcissus* spp.
- Spider Lily — *Lycoris* spp.

Vines

- Wisteria — *Wisteria sinensis*
- Japanese Honeysuckle — *Lonicera japonica*
- English Ivy — *Hedera helix*
- Confederate Star Jasmine — *Trachelospermum jasminoides*

Roses

- Floribunda — *Rosa* 'Europeana'
- Grandiflora — *Rosa* 'Camelot'
- Minatures — *Rosa* 'Jazz Time'
- Old Garden — *Rosa* 'Maiden's Blush'
- Polyantha — *Rosa* 'Cecile Brunner'
- Shrub — *Rosa* 'Bonica'

Trees

- Oak — *Quercus* spp.
- Laceback Elm — *Ulmus parvifolia*
- Chinese Pistachio — *Pistacia chinensis*
- Pine — *Pinus* spp.
- Redbud — *Cercis canadensis*
- Golden Rain Tree *Koelreuteria paniculata*
- Bald Cypress — *Taxodium distichum*

Shrubs

- Holly — *Ilex* spp.
- Crape Myrtle — *Lagerstroemia indica*
- Abelia — *Abelia* x *grandiflora*
- Nandina — *Nandina domestica*
- Indian Hawthorne — *Raphiolepsis indica*
- Althea — *Hibiscus syriacus*
- Boxwood — *Buxus microphylla*
- Camellia — *Camellia japonica*

texas garden favorites

Groundcovers
- Asian Jasmine — *Trachelospermum asiaticum*
- English Ivy — *Hedera helix*
- Monkey Grass — *Liriope muscari*
- Mondo Grass p. — *Ophiopogon japonica*
- Periwinkle — *Vinca major/minor*
- Sedum — *Sedum* spp.
- Wintercreeper — *Euonymus fortunei*

Lawn grasses
- Common Bermuda — *Cynodon dactylon*
- St. Augustine — *Stenotaphrum secundatum*
- Zoysia — *Zoysia japonica*
- Centipede — *Eremochloa ophiuroide*
- Buffalo — *Buchloe dactyloides*

Ornamental grasses
- Monkey Grass — *Liriope muscari*
- Mondo Grass — *Ophiopogon japonica*
- Maidengrass — *Miscanthus sinensis*
- Fountain Grass — *Pennisetum alopecuroides*
- Pampas Grass — *Cortaderia selloana*

Native annuals
- Black-eyed Susan — *Rudbeckia hirta* 'Pulcherrima'
- Indian Blanket — *Gaillardia pulchella*
- Bluebonnet — *Lupinus texensis*
- Clasping-Leaf Coneflower — *Rudbeckia amplexicaulis*
- Plains Coreopsis — *Coreopsis tinctoria*
- Phlox — *Phlox drummondii*
- Indian Paintbrush — *Castilleja indivisa*
- Texas Bluebells — *Eustoma grandiflorum*

Native perennials
- Texas Lantana — *Lantana horrida*
- Mealy Blue Sage — *Salvia farinacea*
- Black-eyed Susan — *Rudbeckia hirta* var. 'Angustifolia'
- Wild Petunia — *Ruellia* spp.
- Mexican Hat. — *Ratibida columnaris*
- Purple Coneflower — *Echinacea augustifolia*
- Evening Primrose — *Oenothera* spp.
- Prairie Verbena — *Verbena bipinnatifida*

Native shrubs
- Texas Sage or Cenizo — *Leucophyllum frutescens*
- American Beautyberry — *Callicarpa americana*
- Wax Myrtle — *Myrica cerifera*
- Salvia Greggii — *Salvia greggii*
- Wooly Butterfly Bush — *Buddleia* spp.

Native trees
- Oak — *Quercus* spp.
- Cedar Elm — *Ulmus crassifolia*
- Pecan — *Carya illinoensis*
- Pine — *Pinus* spp.
- Southern Magnolia — *Magnolia grandiflora*
- Sweet Gum — *Liquidambar styraciflua*
- Flowering Dogwood — *Cornus florida*

Native vines
- Coral Honeysuckle — *Lonicera sempervirens*
- Carolina Jasmine — *Gelsemium sempervirens*
- Passion Vine — *Passiflora incarnata*
- Virginia Creeper — *Parthenocissus quinquefolia*

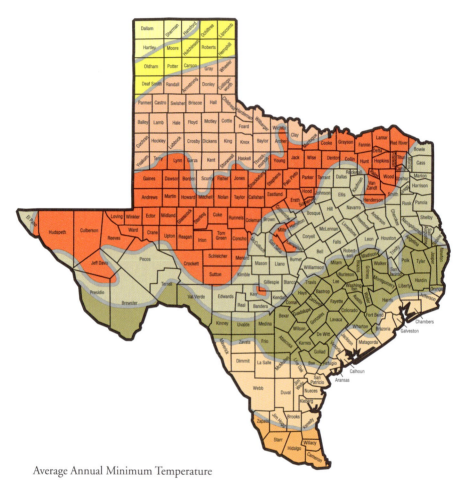

To create a little flower is the labour of ages.

— William Blake

january | week 1
January

garden observations

what's the weather like?

Start the year off right! Photograph your garden at least once every month. This will help you with your planning and planting schemes.

what have I planted/transplanted?

garden notes

What is a weed? A plant whose virtues have not yet been dicovered.

—Ralph Waldo Emerson

tending my garden

january | week 1

january | week 2

January

garden observations

Order seeds now for your favorite annuals, perennials and vegetables. Cut out color photographs and create your own record for what you order.

what's the weather like?

When planning your garden, use a large sheet of graph paper with 1/4 inch grids. A scale of 1 inch = 4 feet is a useful proportion.

what have I planted/transplanted?

garden notes

tending my garden

january | week 2

january | week 3

January

garden observations

what's the weather like?

what have I planted/transplanted?
Cowboy Corner - RADIO

spring of '83 when

403 498 2250

garden notes mention
Preserving Memorie + Making Hast

Cowboy Boots
9434 W Central
Sat 8 AM to Noon

> Check house plants for signs of insects and disease. Spots, speckles or webs on leaves indicate pests are present.

tending my garden

january | week 3

january | week 4

January

garden observations

what's the weather like?

what have I planted/transplanted?

Tip to Remember: You may also use vegetables as ornamental plants. Ornamental peppers and sweet potato vine selections are good examples.

garden notes

tending my garden

january | week 4

february | week 1

February

garden observations

what's the weather like?

Take a walk through your garden, and plan additions to create winter interest for next year.

what have I planted/transplanted?

Did You Know? The only tulip color that has not yet been developed is any shade of blue.

garden notes

tending my garden

february | week 1

february | week 2
February

garden observations

what's the weather like?

what have I planted/transplanted?

> When in doubt, call your local Extension Service. Master Gardeners there will provide information (and the advice is free!)

garden notes

tending my garden

february | week 2

february | week 3

garden observations

Extend the life of your cut flowers. Remove the lower leaves and re-cut the stems before arranging them in lukewarm water.

what's the weather like?

what have I planted/transplanted?

garden notes

Though I do not believe that a plant will spring up where no seed has been, I have great faith in a seed. Convince me that you have a seed there, and I am prepared to expect wonders.

— Henry David Thoreau

tending my garden

february | week 3

february | week 4

February

garden observations

what's the weather like?

Tip to Remember: Fill clear plastic milk jugs with water and place around young tomato plants. They will provide warmth overnight for young plants, helping you get a jump on spring.

what have I planted/transplanted?

garden notes

tending my garden

february | week 4

march | week 1

March

Direct sow wildflower seeds where you want them to grow in climates with USDA zones 1 through 6. (Check the zone map in the introduction to identify your zone.)

Take a soil test now so you will know how to prepare your garden for the next season.

what's blooming?

what's the weather like?

what have I planted/transplanted?

garden notes

tending my garden

march | week 1

march | week 2

what's blooming?

Tip to Remember: Plan to add a few annuals to your perennial garden to help provide season-long blooms.

what's the weather like?

Watch for aphids on shrubs as they leaf out. Treat with insecticidal soap or any other labeled pesticide, if needed.

what have I planted/transplanted?

Start tomato seeds for transplants 4-6 weeks before optimum planting time in your area.

garden notes

tending my garden

march | week 2

march | week 3

March

Single-flower forms of marigolds and zinnias are more appealing to butterflies than the double-flower forms.

Did You Know? Viburnum is a member of the honeysuckle family.

what's blooming?

what's the weather like?

what have I planted/transplanted?

garden notes

tending my garden

march | week 3

march | week 4

March

what's blooming?

what's the weather like?

> Hummingbirds love tubular flowers such as trumpet vine, coral honeysuckle, and nicotiana. Plant lots of these if you want to attract hummingbirds.

what have I planted/transplanted?

garden notes

tending my garden

march | week 4

Half the interest of a garden is the constant exercise of the imagination.

— C.W. Earle

april | week 1

what's blooming?

what's the weather like?

Have you photographed your garden lately? This will help with your garden planning and design ideas.

An easy time to weed is the day after a gentle rain, when the soil is slightly moist, and weeds are easy to pull—roots and all.

what have I planted/transplanted?

garden notes

tending my garden

april | week 1

april | week 2

Propagate some of your favorite broadleaf shrubs using this simple layering technique: Select a branch that is close to the ground. Bend the branch so that it is in contact with the soil. Cover the branch with soil. Water well and hold the branch in place with a brick. In six weeks, check to see if there are roots. Once the roots are firmly established, cut the new plant off from the mother plant.

what's blooming?

what's the weather like?

what have I planted/transplanted?

garden notes

tending my garden

april | week 2

As is the gardener, such is the garden.

— Hebrew Proverb

april | week 3

what's blooming?

Tip to Remember: When digging a hole for a tree, it's best to dig the hole at least half again as wide as the size of the rootball (much wider is even better). Use the same soil you dug out to backfill around the rootball and water-in well.

what's the weather like?

Turn your compost pile. If you haven't started one already, call your Extension Service for advice.

what have I planted/transplanted?

garden notes

tending my garden

april | week 3

april | week 4

what's blooming?

what's the weather like?

Wooden clothespins can be used as plant markers.

Place grow-thru stakes above plants that need support in early spring, and in a short time they will cover the stakes.

what have I planted/transplanted?

garden notes

tending my garden

april | week 4

may week 1

Plan to prune back spring-blooming azaleas and other shrubs such as forsythia or spirea after they finish flowering. This way you won't cut off any potential flower buds for next year.

Check plants once or twice a week for insect and disease problems. It's easier to control a small infestation if it's discovered early.

what's blooming?

what's the weather like?

what have I planted/transplanted?

garden notes

tending my garden

may | week 1

may / week 2

May

what's blooming?

what's the weather like?

> Incorporate a slow-release fertilizer in the soil of hanging baskets and container plantings. This will provide nutrients for several months in one application.

what have I planted/transplanted?

tending my garden

garden notes

Many diseases can be controlled with sanitation. Remove and destroy any infected leaves as soon as they are found.

may | week 2

may week 3

what's blooming?

what's the weather like?

Parsley and fennel provide food for butterfly caterpillars.

Interest children in gardening by planning a small child's garden. A bean tee-pee is fun to plant and grow!

what have I planted/transplanted?

garden notes

> The best time for slug hunting is at night using a flashlight and a pair of gloves.

tending my garden

may | week 3

May

may | week 4

Did You Know? Bees are our most efficient pollinators for flowers, fruits, and vegetables. Any garden with lots of bees is a healthy environment.

what's blooming?

what's the weather like?

what have I planted/transplanted?

garden notes

tending my garden

Tickle it with a hoe and it will laugh into a harvest.

—English Proverb

may | week 4

june | week 1

A perennial garden looks wonderful when planted against a background of a wall, a hedge, or evergreen shrubs.

A plant's scientific name consists of a genus and an epithet. The genus and the epithet are always italicized and the genus begins with a capital letter. A third word in the name may refer to a specific variety, called a cultivar. It is set off by single quotation marks.

what's blooming?

what's the weather like?

2000 HOT

what have I planted/transplanted?

garden notes

2000 3rd - John put down Medina (2nd x) & cedarcide
Sighted hummingbird at front feeder / 4th 1" RAIN

tending my garden

june | week 1

june | week 2

what's blooming?

Use vines to create vertical interest in the garden. If you don't have a wall or fence on which to train them, a lattice or arbor will work.

what's the weather like?

You can create your own portable seep irrigation system by punching a few holes in plastic containers and placing them beside plants that need additional moisture.

what have I planted/transplanted?

garden notes

tending my garden

june | week 2

Though an old man, I am but a young gardener...

—Thomas Jefferson

june | week 3

June

> Plan to shear fall-blooming asters to make them bushier and more compact.

what's blooming?

what's the weather like?

Did You Know? Even though a plant may be identified as self-cleaning, flowers are better off if you deadhead, or remove the spent blooms as often as you can. This will allow the plant to use its energy to make more flowers and leaves instead of making seeds.

what have I planted/transplanted?

garden notes

tending my garden

june | week 3

june week 4

what's blooming?

what's the weather like?

BTK (*Bacillus thuringiensis kurstaki*) is an organic biological control that is effective against many caterpillars and is safe to use on vegetable crops. *Bacillus thuringiensis* 'San Diego' is effective against some leafeating beetles.

what have I planted/transplanted?

garden notes

tending my garden

june | week 4

july week 1

Harvest herbs for drying as soon as they come into flower. Bundle them up with a rubber band and hang them on a line in a dark, dry place with good air circulation. To preserve the best flavor once they are dry, store the herbs in airtight containers away from heat and light.

Press some flowers and add to this journal. It's a pretty record of what you planted.

what's blooming?

what's the weather like?

what have I planted/transplanted?

garden notes

tending my garden

july | week 1

july week 2

what's blooming?

what's the weather like?

what have I planted/transplanted?

Deadhead hybrid tea roses throughout the summer to encourage more blooms.

garden notes

tending my garden

july | week 2

july week 3

what's blooming?

---

what's the weather like?

> Most unwanted summer heat comes through east- and west-facing windows, not through well-insulated roofs and walls. Plant a deciduous tree for shade.

what have I planted/transplanted?

garden notes

tending my garden

july | week 3

july week 4

Plants use calcium to build strong cell walls and stems. Deficiencies can cause blossom-end rot on tomatoes.

Did You Know? The Greeks and Romans used lavender in bath water. In fact, the Latin name "lavare" means, "wash".

Tip to Remember: When planting seeds, position them in geometric patterns so that you will be able to distinguish them more easily from weed seedlings.

what's blooming?

what's the weather like?

what have I planted/transplanted?

garden notes

tending my garden

Gardening is the purest of human pleasures.
—Francis Bacon

july | week 4

august week 1

what's blooming?

what's the weather like?

Preserve basil leaves by mixing them in the blender with a small amount of water. Fill ice cube trays with the mixture. Once they freeze, put them in freezer bags. This way you will have basil to use in your favorite Italian dishes all winter long.

what have I planted/transplanted?

garden notes

tending my garden

august | week 1

august | week 2

what's blooming?

For the best selection, order your spring-flowering bulbs or purchase them locally when they become available in your area. Keep them cool and dry until you plant them.

what's the weather like?

Take some photographs of your garden to refer to later when planning for next year.

what have I planted/transplanted?

garden notes

tending my garden

august | week 2

august week 3

If you haven't already done so, draw a plan of your property showing existing trees and shrubs in relation to your house. Make notes throughout the year indicating those areas that receive full sun, shade or a mix of sun and shade. This will help you to choose the right plant for the right place.

what's blooming?

what's the weather like?

what have I planted/transplanted?

garden notes

tending my garden

august | week 3

august week 4

August

what's blooming?

Water your compost pile when the weather has been dry.

what's the weather like?

Order three or four types of paperwhite narcissus to force at two-week intervals. You will have flowers from Halloween into the New Year!

what have I planted/transplanted?

Continue to harvest vegetables as soon as they are ripe. Regular harvesting increases production.

garden notes

He who plants a garden plants happiness.
—Chinese Proverb

tending my garden

august | week 4

september week 1

what's blooming?

what's the weather like?

Expand your plant collection by exchanging seeds and plants with fellow gardeners.

what have I planted/transplanted?

Add some shrubs to your garden that will offer winter interest such as colorful bark, or unusual shapes.

garden notes

tending my garden

september | week 1

september | week 2

what's blooming?

what's the weather like?

If you haven't started one already, begin a compost pile and let it overwinter. In six months you should have "black gold" to mix into your garden.

what have I planted/transplanted?

garden notes

The frost hurts not weeds.
— Thomas Fuller

tending my garden

september | week 2

september | week 3

what's blooming?

what's the weather like?

what have I planted/transplanted?

garden notes

If your annuals are beginning to look ragged, pull them and replace with some mums, pansies, or flowering kale.

september | week 4

Use dried seed heads such as sedum and lotus for fall decorations.

Visit your favorite nursery to select a tree or shrub for that spot in the garden that needs something new.

what's blooming?

what's the weather like?

what have I planted/transplanted?

garden notes

tending my garden

september | week 4

october | week 1

what's blooming?

what's the weather like?

Plant a tree in honor of a birth or in memory of a loved one.

Fall leaf color is triggered by cooler temperatures, shorter days, and less light.

what have I planted/transplanted?

garden notes

tending my garden

october | week 1

october | week 2
October

what's blooming?

what's the weather like?

what have I planted/transplanted?

garden notes

> Sprinkle annual rye grass seed on top of the soil of pots you are forcing. By the time the bulbs bloom, it will create a green carpet underneath them.

tending my garden

october | week 2

october | week 3

what's blooming?

what's the weather like?

Tip to Remember: Parsley is a good plant for bed edges. It also looks great grown in containers with pansies.

Use golf tees to mark areas where bulbs are planted.

what have I planted/transplanted?

garden notes

> *Heaven is under our feet as well as over our heads.*
> —Henry David Thoreau

tending my garden

october | week 3

october | week 4

what's blooming?

what's the weather like?

Did You Know? The word 'wort', as in St. John's Wort, is an old English term that means "medicinal plant".

what have I planted/transplanted?

garden notes

tending my garden

october | week 4

november | week 1

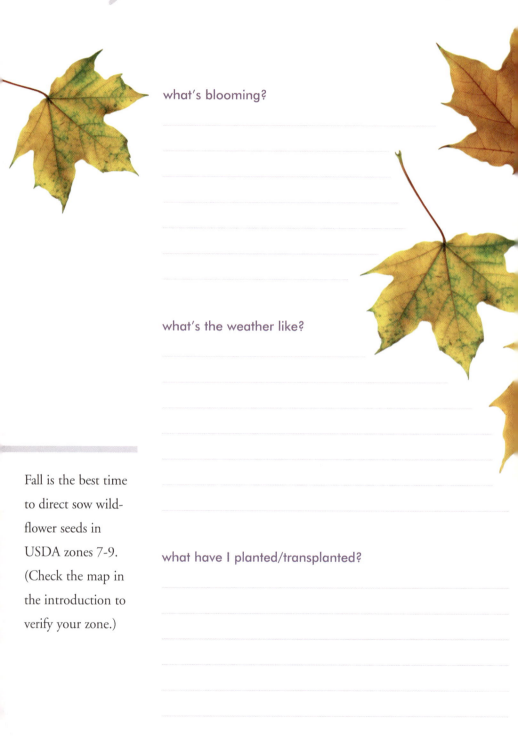

what's blooming?

what's the weather like?

Fall is the best time to direct sow wildflower seeds in USDA zones 7-9. (Check the map in the introduction to verify your zone.)

what have I planted/transplanted?

garden notes

tending my garden

november | week 1

Autumn is a second spring when every leaf is a flower. —Albert Camus

november | week 2

November

what's blooming?

what's the weather like?

Continue to mow your lawn for as long as it keeps growing.

Clean and sharpen garden tools. Lightly coat with oil to prevent rust.

what have I planted/transplanted?

garden notes

tending my garden

november | week 2

november | week 3

November

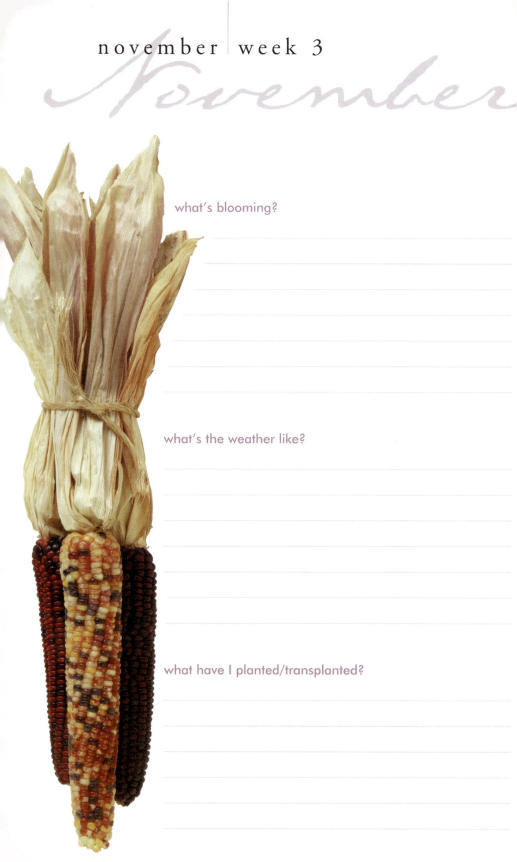

what's blooming?

what's the weather like?

what have I planted/transplanted?

garden notes

Extend the life of your fresh-cut holiday tree by storing it in a cool shady place until you move it indoors. Re-cut the trunk before moving it indoors and use plenty of fresh water in the reservoir.

tending my garden

november | week 3

november | week 4

For best results, store unused seeds in a cool, dark place in an air- and water-resistant container.

Selecting the right tool for the job can prevent most injuries. Wear safety gear when operating power equipment.

what's blooming?

what's the weather like?

what have I planted/transplanted?

garden notes

tending my garden

november | week 4

december | week 1

Make a wreath for the holidays. Rose hips, bittersweet, and euonymus are good choices for materials.

garden observations

what's the weather like?

what have I planted/ transplanted?

garden notes

A garden is a friend you can visit any time.
—unknown

tending my garden

december | week 1

december | week 2

garden observations

Cast iron plant, Chinese evergreen, heartleaf philodendron, and snake plant will tolerate low-light conditions.

what's the weather like?

Tip to Remember: The winter sun provides the most solar heat through south-facing windows. Avoid planting shade trees or evergreens that may shade these heat-absorbing windows if you need the extra warmth.

what have I planted/transplanted?

garden notes

tending my garden

december | week 2

december | week 3

Recycle your holiday tree. The branches can be removed and used as mulch. Or you can leave the tree intact and use it as a windbreak and shelter for birds.

Don't put wood ashes in your compost pile; they will alter the pH level too much.

garden observations

what's the weather like?

what have I planted/transplanted?

garden notes

tending my garden

december | week 3

december | week 4

garden observations

what's the weather like?

what have I planted/transplanted?

garden notes

> Pruning large trees, especially those located near utilities should be performed by a professional. Call a certified arborist if you need trees pruned.

tending my garden

december | week 4

plant inventory/history

name

when planted

where planted

size

source

price

name

when planted

where planted

size

source

price

name

when planted

where planted

size

source

price

name

when planted

where planted

size

source

price

name

when planted

where planted

size

source

price

name

when planted

where planted

size

source

price

name

when planted

where planted

size

source

price

name

when planted

where planted

size

source

price

plant inventory/history

name

when planted

where planted

size

source

price

name

when planted

where planted

size

source

price

name

when planted

where planted

size

source

price

name

when planted

where planted

size

source

price

name

when planted

where planted

size

source

price

name

when planted

where planted

size

source

price

name

when planted

where planted

size

source

price

name

when planted

where planted

size

source

price

plant inventory/history

name

when planted

where planted

size

source

price

name

when planted

where planted

size

source

price

name

when planted

where planted

size

source

price

name

when planted

where planted

size

source

price

name

when planted

where planted

size

source

price

name

when planted

where planted

size

source

price

name

when planted

where planted

size

source

price

name

when planted

where planted

size

source

price

plant inventory/history

name

when planted

where planted

size

source

price

name

when planted

where planted

size

source

price

name

when planted

where planted

size

source

price

name

when planted

where planted

size

source

price

name

when planted

where planted

size

source

price

name

when planted

where planted

size

source

price

name

when planted

where planted

size

source

price

name

when planted

where planted

size

source

price

plant inventory/history

name

when planted

where planted

size

source

price

---

name

when planted

where planted

size

source

price

---

name

when planted

where planted

size

source

price

---

name

when planted

where planted

size

source

price

---

name

when planted

where planted

size

source

price

---

name

when planted

where planted

size

source

price

---

name

when planted

where planted

size

source

price

---

name

when planted

where planted

size

source

price

plant inventory/history

name

when planted

where planted

size

source

price

name

when planted

where planted

size

source

price

name

when planted

where planted

size

source

price

name

when planted

where planted

size

source

price

name

when planted

where planted

size

source

price

name

when planted

where planted

size

source

price

name

when planted

where planted

size

source

price

name

when planted

where planted

size

source

price

plant inventory/history

name	name
when planted	when planted
where planted	where planted
size	size
source	source
price	price
name	name
when planted	when planted
where planted	where planted
size	size
source	source
price	price
name	name
when planted	when planted
where planted	where planted
size	size
source	source
price	price
name	name
when planted	when planted
where planted	where planted
size	size
source	source
price	price

plant inventory/history

name	**name**
when planted	when planted
where planted	where planted
size	size
source	source
price	price
name	**name**
when planted	when planted
where planted	where planted
size	size
source	source
price	price
name	**name**
when planted	when planted
where planted	where planted
size	size
source	source
price	price
name	**name**
when planted	when planted
where planted	where planted
size	size
source	source
price	price

my garden plan

my garden plan

suppliers & resources

suppliers and resources

photos

photos